you've got a friend

Compiled by
Dan Zadra

Designed by
Clarie Yam

COMPENDIUM™
INCORPORATED

live inspired.

Acknowledgements

These quotations were gathered lovingly but unscientifically over several years and/or were contributed by many friends or acquaintances. Some arrived—and survived in our files—on scraps of paper and may therefore be imperfectly worded or attributed. To the authors, contributors and original sources, our thanks, and where appropriate, our apologies. –The Editors

With Special Thanks To

Jason Aldrich, Gerry Baird, Jay Baird, Neil Beaton, Josie Bissett, Laura Boro, Melissa Carlson, M.H. Clark, Tiffany Parente Connors, Jim & Alyssa Darragh & Family, Rob Estes, Pamela Farrington, Michael & Leianne Flynn & Family, Sarah Forster, Liz Heinlein & Family, Renee & Brad Holmes, Jennifer Hurwitz, Heidi Jones, Sheila Kamuda, Michelle Kim, Carol Anne Kennedy, June Martin, David Miller, Carin Moore & Family, Moose, Jessica Phoenix & Tom DesLongchamp, Janet Potter & Family, Joanna Price, Heidi & Jose Rodriguez, Diane Roger, Alie Satterlee, Kirsten & Garrett Sessions, Andrea Summers, Brien Thompson, Helen Tsao, Anne Whiting, Kobi & Heidi Yamada & Family, Justi and Tote Yamada & Family, Bob & Val Yamada, Kaz & Kristin Yamada & Family, Tai & Joy Yamada, Anne Zadra, August & Arline Zadra, and Gus & Rosie Zadra.

Credits

Compiled by Dan Zadra
Designed by Steve Potter and Clarie Yam

ISBN: 978-1-932319-23-1

Printed in China

thoughts to
celebrate the joy
of **friendship**

you've got a friend

No friendship, however brief,
can cross the path of our destiny without
leaving some mark on it forever.

—François Mauriac

An old proverb says that "one friend in a lifetime is much; two are many; and three are hardly possible." Not so! The truth is, starting when we're little kids and continuing to the very end, good friends have a way of materializing in (and out) of our lives at every turn.

First come our childhood friends, then our high school and college friends, and then the friends we work with, or raise our families with, or do our community service with, and then come the friends after that, and on it goes. True, maybe just one, two or three of those friends come to stay forever, while the rest come and go. But each and every friendship, however brief, brings a lasting and priceless gift, if we will only stop to look for it.

"It sometimes seems like I am Grand Central Station," wrote author Vickie Girard. "I stay in place as so many pass in and out of my life. We spend special time together during the chaotic interim until they are once again on a train. Yes, sometimes the farewells are sad, but while they are at the station, what a time we've had."

Think of all the wonderful people in your own station in life and be happy for them; honor them. What a time you've had! Don't wait for tomorrow to tell them how you feel. Let them know today, "You've got a friend."

Dan Zadra

Friendship?
Yes, please.

Charles Dickens

There is no such thing
as common friendship.

Kelly Ann Rothaus

One does not make friends.
One recognizes them.

Irene Dunn

People come into your life
for a reason, a season or a lifetime.
When you figure out which it is,
you know exactly what to do.

Michelle Ventor

you've got a **friend**

Some friendships
are created by nature,
some by interest,
and some by souls.

Jeremy Taylor

Who shall explain
the extraordinary instinct that tells us,
perhaps after a single meeting, that this
or that particular person in some
mysterious way matters to us?

A.C. Benson

you've got a **friend**

How can it be, except by the
miracle of friendship, that someone
can know you so well even though
you have told him virtually
nothing about your life?

Carlos Menta

Love is blind.
Friendship is clairvoyant.

Philippe Soupault

you've got a **friend**

A friend is someone
who reaches for your hand...
and touches your heart.

Unknown

What comes from the heart,
goes to the heart.

Samuel Taylor Coleridge

Friendship blossoms when
two people say to each other,
in effect: "What? You too?
I thought I was the only one!"

C.S. Lewis

you've got a **friend**

The friend
given to you by circumstances
over which you have no control
was God's own gift.

Frederick Robertson

Long sought,
rarely found,
and forever kept.

"True Friends"

you've got a **friend**

When you're with a friend,
your heart has come home.

Emily Farrar

Oh, the comfort, the inexpressible
comfort of feeling safe with a person,
having neither to weigh thoughts nor
measure words but to pour them all out,
just as it is, chaff and grain together,
knowing that a faithful hand will take
and sift them, keeping what is worth
keeping, and then, with the breath
of kindness, blow the rest away.

George Eliot

you've got a **friend**

A friend is what
the heart needs all the time.

Henry van Dyke

One good heart
attracts another. Each true friend
deserves the other.

Shaker Saying

It is the friendship of good people
that is friendship most of all.

Aristotle

you've got a **friend**

Each person represents
a world in us, a world possibly
not born until they arrive, and
it is only by this meeting that
a new world is born.

Anaïs Nin

It was the excitement
of making a new best friend—
the best, the purest feeling
I've ever known.

Keith Hale

you've got a **friend**

Friendship is
a great place.
I'm glad we're here.
Cat Davis

Whatever
souls are made of—
yours and mine
are the same.
Emily Brontë

"Friend. GOOD!"
Frankenstein's Monster

you've got a **friend**

My fondest memories are of my friends.

Tote Yamada

Remembering is
a dream that comes in waves.

Helga Sandberg

In my heart are all the
treasures that I shall ever own:
they are the memories of all
the old friends I have known.

Kimberly Knutsen

I trace my roots,
not to my ancestors, but
to my childhood friends.

Carlos Menta

you've got a **friend**

I don't remember how
we happened to meet each other,
I don't remember who got along with
whom first. All I can remember is
all of us together, always.

The Friendship Page

There has always been,
and there will probably always be,
the three of us crashing through life
together—thick and thin. Our parents used
to call us the "wrecktangle."

Lorna Greene

you've got a **friend**

We set off for school side by side, our feet in step, not touching but feeling as if we were joined at the shoulder, hip, ankle, not to mention heart.

Jamaica Kincaid

You know how kids choose up sides for kickball. Well, Jerry Elliot was probably the first and only kid who ever picked me first. Thirty years later we're still great friends.

Frank Blass

you've got a **friend**

So we just wandered off along the path
behind the school. We really weren't going
anywhere, but when we felt like running,
we just ran. The day was like that, and the
things we did just happened. And somehow,
that made them seem more special—
like something from a dream...

Zilpha Keatley Snyder

20

My parents would only allow
brown bread and low-fat margarine
in the house. On summer days, my best
friends and I would sneak loaves of stark
white Wonder Bread, toast it all up
and slather it with real butter.

Deborah Snow

you've got a **friend**

We were so naive as kids that
we used to sneak behind the barn
and do nothing.

Johnny Carson

We have a special bond. We're the
only two left in our circle of childhood
pals who haven't had breast implants.

Phoebe Whorley

Time—our youth—it never really goes,
does it? It is all held in our minds.

Helen Santmyer

you've got a **friend**

Never lose your child's heart.

Mencius

I was wise enough
to never grow up while fooling
most people into believing I had.

Margaret Mead

It is not that we belong to the past,
but that the past belongs to us.

Mary Antin

you've got a **friend**

What people
need is a good
listening to.

Mary Lou Casey

Friends are those rare people
who ask how we are, and then
wait to hear the answer.

Ed Cunningham

There is a definite process
by which one makes people
into friends, and it involves talking
to them and listening to them
for hours at a time.

Rebecca West

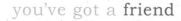

you've got a **friend**

The soul selects
her own society.

Emily Dickinson

A soul friend is someone
with whom we can share our
greatest joys and deepest fears,
confess our worst sins and most
persistent faults, clarify our
highest hopes and perhaps
most unarticulated dreams.

Edward C. Sellner

you've got a **friend**

Something we were
withholding made us weak...
Until we found it was ourselves.

Robert Frost

Cut out those
intimate little dinners for two—
unless there's someone with you.

Joey Adams

Happiness is not perfected
until it is shared.

Jane Porter

you've got a **friend**

God, I've been starving
for this kind of conversation!

Eleanor Coppola

There was no way for me
to understand it at the time,
but the talk that filled the kitchen
those afternoons served as therapy,
the cheapest kind available to my mother
and her friends. But more than therapy,
that freewheeling, wide-ranging,
exuberant talk functioned as an
outlet for the tremendous creative
energy they possessed.

Paula Marshall

you've got a **friend**

Everyone old enough to
have a secret is entitled to have
some special people to keep it with.

Sarah Baker

The silver friend knows
your present, and the gold friend
knows all your past dirt and glories.
Once in a blue moon there's someone
who knows it all, someone who knows
and accepts you unconditionally,
someone who's there for life.

Jill McCorkle

you've got a **friend**

Eventually, it's the silences
which make the real conversations
between friends. Not the saying,
but the never needing to say.

Margaret Lee Runbeck

There's no need to say,
"It's been a great day" when
we say good-bye. We just wave
a hand and we understand.

"Reminiscences"

you've got a **friend**

If somebody believes
in you, and you believe
in your dreams,
it can happen.

Tiffany Rowe

There comes that mysterious
meeting in life when someone
acknowledges who we are and what
we can be, igniting the circuits
of our highest potential.

Rusty Berkus

My best friend is
the one who brings out
the best in me.

Henry Ford

Anything, everything, little or big
becomes an adventure when
the right person shares it.

Kathleen Norris

you've got a **friend**

We are so much less
without each other.

What one cannot,
another can.

32

While the right friends
are near us, we feel that all is well.
Our everyday life blossoms suddenly
into bright possibilities.

you've got a **friend**

We is terrific.

Diana Ross

People must believe
in each other, and feel
that it can be done and
must be done; in that way
they are enormously strong.
We must keep up each
other's courage.

Vincent van Gogh

you've got a **friend**

Thank you for
believing in me before
I believed in myself.

Kobi Yamada

Sometimes our light goes out
but is blown into flame by another
human being. Each of us owes
deepest thanks to those who
have rekindled this light.

Albert Schweitzer

you've got a **friend**

Everywhere, we learn best
from those whom we love.

Someone saw
something in you once.
That's partly why you are
where you are today. Whoever
it was had the kindness and the
foresight to bet on your future.
Today, take 10 minutes to write a
grateful note to the person who
helped you. You'll keep a
wonderful friendship alive.

you've got a **friend**

There are people who
take the heart out of you,
and there are people who
put it back.

Elizabeth David

36

Why, I don't know—but,
I always like myself better when
I'm with my friends. Somehow,
they pull the best from me,
effortlessly, weightlessly.

Jeri Burnett

you've got a **friend**

Perhaps friendship is
the process of my leading you
gently back to yourself.

Antoine de Saint Exupéry

To love a person is
to learn the song that
is in their heart, and to
sing it to them when they
have forgotten.

Thomas Chandler

you've got a **friend**

We all need to be
recognized for what we're doing,
for our work. Every once in a while
we need someone to come up to us
and say, "You're beautiful. That was
well done. That's nice."

Leo Buscaglia

There is only one real deprivation,
I decided this morning, and that is
not to be able to give one's gifts
to those one loves most.

May Sarton

you've got a **friend**

Moreover, in loving
their friend they love what
is good for themselves.

Aristotle

It's a great satisfaction
knowing that for a brief point in time
you made a difference.

Irene Natividad

We are rich only
through what we give,
and poor only through
what we refuse.

Ann-Sophie Swetchine

you've got a **friend**

People who love us
for what we are, not for what
we have done, are precious support
when we're trying to do and be more.

Peter McWilliams

I love you, not only
for what you are, but for
what I am when I am with you.
I love you, not only for what
you have made of yourself, but for
what you are making of me.

Elizabeth Barrett Browning

you've got a **friend**

All we have to do
to be successful is follow the
advice we give others.

Dear Abby

Nothing is so embarrassing as
watching your friend do something
you told him couldn't be done.

Calvin Peete

If at first you don't succeed,
you'll probably have more friends.

Whoopi Goldberg

you've got a **friend**

One can't really play
with her friends in a tiara.

The worst part of success
is to try to find someone who
is happy for you.

If I'm such a legend,
why am I so lonely?

you've got a **friend**

Winning has always
meant much to me, but winning
friends has meant the most.

Babe Didrikson Zaharias

To laugh often and much,
to win the respect of intelligent
people and the affection of children...
to leave the world a bit better...
to know even one life has breathed
easier because you have lived,
that is to have succeeded.

Ralph Waldo Emerson

you've got a **friend**

Keep shining,
my bright and shining star of a friend.

Ivy Baker

Grow into your perfection.

Kobi Yamada

Never let anyone steal your dream.
It's your dream, not theirs!

Dan Zadra

you've got a **friend**

A friend walks in
when the whole world
walks out.

Walter Winchell

In prosperity our friends know us;
in adversity we know our friends.

J. Churton Collins

Lots of people want to ride
with you in the limo, but what
you want is someone who will
take the bus with you when
the limo breaks down.

Oprah Winfrey

Some people we can always depend
upon for making the best, instead of the
worst, of whatever happens.

Sandra Wilde

you've got a **friend**

Love is what you've
been through with somebody.

James Thurber

We have been friends together
in sunshine and shade.

Caroline Norton

I didn't know,
until I was at odds with the world,
how much my friends who believe
in me...mean to me.

D.H. Lawrence

you've got a **friend**

Crises do not make friends,
they reveal them.

The object is not to
see through one another, but
to see one another through.

Friendship is two hearts
pulling at one load.

you've got a **friend**

"That would be nice."

Charlie Brown,
on hearing that in life you win some and lose some

How can there be so much
difference between a day off
and an off day?

Doug Larson

My friend Betsy will say,
"I don't know whose life I hate more—
yours or mine." It makes us laugh.

Francine Russo

you've got a **friend**

We might as well live.

Since the house is on fire
let us warm ourselves.

If you're already walking on thin ice,
why not dance?

you've got a **friend**

The world knows nothing
of its greatest people.

Henry Taylor

It's the friends you can call up
at 4 A.M. that matter.

Marlene Dietrich

I could do without
many things with no hardship—
you are not one of them.

Ashleigh Brilliant

you've got a **friend**

Friendship
glows in the dark.

Cat Lane

Trouble is a part of life,
and if you don't share it, you don't give
the person who loves you a chance
to love you enough.

Dinah Shore

People say I've had a hard life,
but I've also had very good
company along the way.

Helen Keller

you've got a **friend**

Nothing lasts forever,
not even your troubles.

Mileposts

Our friendship will endure
as long as you wish it to.

Barbara Armand

The hard times
we go through will lead to
the good times we'll have.

Henry Littlefield

you've got a **friend**

I think we're here
for each other.

Carol Burnett

The best thing
to hold onto in life
is each other.

Audrey Hepburn

Some people make the world
more special just by being in it.

Kelly Ann Rothaus

'Twas her thinking of others
made you think of her.

Elizabeth Barrett Browning

you've got a **friend**

Caring is everything.

Treasure the one
who thinks of you when all others
are thinking of themselves.

It is lovely,
when I forget all birthdays,
including my own, to find that
somebody remembers me.

you've got a **friend**

When friends ask,
there is no tomorrow...
only now.

Alexander Drey

If a friend is in trouble,
don't annoy him by asking if
there is anything you can do.
Make up something appropriate
and do it!

Edgar Howe

you've got a **friend**

Go ahead and cry,
I'll catch your tears.

Jileen Russell

The love of our friend in all its fullness
simply means being able to say to him,
"What are you going through?"

Simone Weil

Measure your friends
around the heart.

English proverb

you've got a **friend**

For many people in this world,
life is cold, lonely and hard. If they had
one friend, their lives would not only
be different, but happier. In the plan of
God, a friendship is a touch of heaven
on earth. And we can all bring a touch
of heaven into someone's life.

Rev. Mark Connolly   59

If someone listens,
or stretches out a hand, or whispers
a kind word of encouragement, or
attempts to understand, extraordinary
things begin to happen.

Loretta Girzartis

you've got a **friend**

When I take you in my life,
I now have four arms instead of two.
Two heads. Four legs. Two possibilities
for joy. Sure, two possibilities for tears,
but I can be there for you while you cry
and you can be there while I cry,
because nobody should ever cry alone.

Leo Buscaglia

Everyone stands alone
on the heart of the earth
pierced by a ray of sunlight:
and suddenly it is evening.

Salvatore Quasimodo

you've got a **friend**

And remember, we all
stumble, every one of us.
That's why it's a comfort
to go hand in hand.

Emily Kimbrough

Lean on me
when you're not strong,
and I'll be your friend,
I'll help you carry on,
for it won't be long
'til I'm going to need
somebody to lean on.

Bill Withers

you've got a **friend**

Ah! How good it feels,
the hand of an old friend.

When someone hugs you,
let them be the first to let go.

How beautiful it is to be able
to say to someone, "I need you."
We think to be a grownup we must be
independent and not need anyone—and
that's why we're all dying of loneliness!
How wonderful to be needed!

you've got a **friend**

Our greatest duty and our
main duty is to help others, and please,
if you can't help them, would you
please not hurt them?

the Dalai Lama

What could I have done
to have saved someone in my life?

Arthur Miller

Take good care of yourself,
just as you have taken such good
care of others.

Dan Zadra

you've got a **friend**

We will always
have time for the
things we put first.

Liane Steele

Let us pause to warm
our hands before the fire of life.

Walter Landor

Who puts the coffee on for two.
Who makes me laugh when I am blue.
No matter what I have to do—
My friend, there's always time for you.

Unknown

No day ends if it makes a memory.

Jackie Erickson

you've got a **friend**

You must be present to win.

No matter what troubles or
travails may loom ahead for you,
do not let yourself be cheated
out of the joy and beauty of today.

Henry Ward Beecher

No one has time;
we have to make time.

James Rhoen

you've got a **friend**

Nobody sees a flower really;
it is so small. We haven't time,
and to see takes time—like to
have a friend takes time.

Georgia O'Keeffe

When just being together is
more important than what you do,
you are with a friend.

Stephanie James

She took me to lunch even when
I wasn't tax deductible.

"Reminiscences"

you've got a **friend**

We don't recognize the most
significant moments in our lives
until they are past us.

Moonlight Graham,
"Field of Dreams"

I would rather have 30 minutes
of "wonderful" than a lifetime of
nothing special.

Julia Roberts

Open your mind, open your heart,
open your arms, take it all in.

Kobi Yamada

you've got a **friend**

The best way to pay for
a lovely moment is to enjoy it.

In the end, what affects your
life most deeply are things too
simple to talk about.

Hold out your hands
to feel the luxury of the sunbeams.

you've got a **friend**

There's no time
like the pleasant.

Oliver Herford

The greatest lesson from the mystics
is that the sacred is in the ordinary,
that it is to be found in one's daily life,
in one's neighbors, friends, and family,
in one's back yard.

Abraham H. Maslow

Count each day a separate life.

Seneca

you've got a **friend**

You can get lonesome—
being that busy.

Isabel Lennart

For the sake of making a living
we forget to live.

Margaret Fuller

Work is the greatest thing
in the world. So you should save
some of it for tomorrow.

Don Herold

you've got a **friend**

I shall tell you a great secret,
my friend. Do not wait for the last
judgment, it takes place every day.

Albert Camus

We really need only
five things on this earth:
Some food, some sun, some work,
some fun and someone.

Beatrice Nolan

Nothing is worth more
than this day.

Johann Wolfgang von Goethe

you've got a **friend**

People are more fun than anybody.

Dorothy Parker

Life is a lot more amusing
than we thought.

That is the best—to laugh
with someone because you both think
the same things are funny.

Laughter is
the best communion of all.

you've got a **friend**

There are souls in this world
who have the gift of finding joy
everywhere—and leaving it
behind them when they go.

Frederick William Faber

It's hard to imagine things without
her, you know, because every now and
then it's like, you know, I've gotta hear
that laugh that she does. I've just gotta
hear that. It's like craving your
favorite food or something.

The Friends Network

you've got a **friend**

Life is too important
to be taken seriously.

Oscar Wilde

Anything worth taking seriously
is worth making fun of.

Tom Lehrer

It is bad to suppress laughter.
It goes back down and spreads
to your hips.

Fred Allen

you've got a **friend**

The joy of living
was meant to be shared.
Happiness was born a twin.

Don Ward

Take time every day
to do something ridiculous.

Philipa Walker

Life is too short to be cranky.

Beej Whiteaker-Hawks

you've got a **friend**

Procrastination is fun.
Just wait and see.

Graffito

How beautiful it is to do nothing,
and then to rest afterward.

Spanish proverb

When you start to look like
your passport picture—you know
you need a vacation.

Unknown

you've got a **friend**

I finally figured out the
main reason to be alive is to enjoy it.

Rita Mae Brown

We're always being told
that time is running out; it is and
getting things done won't stop it.

Joan Silber

There's never enough time
to do all the nothing you want.

Bill Watterson

you've got a **friend**

Boredom arises from routine.
Joy, wonder, rapture, arise from
surprise. Routine leads to boredom
and if we are bored, we are boring.

Leo Buscaglia

Keep smiling—It makes
people wonder what you're up to.

Bob Dolfay

Enjoy yourself.
If you can't enjoy yourself,
enjoy someone else.

Jack Schaefer

you've got a **friend**

We have one
thing in common.
Each of us brings
to our lives a certain
amount of mess.

Francis Ford Coppola

My friend is not perfect,
no more than I,
and so we suit each other
admirably.

82

I've only met four
perfect people in my life and
I didn't like any of them.

It isn't easy being green.

A friend is someone
you want to be around when
you feel like being by yourself.

Nobody's looking,
so there's no more need
to be normal.

you've got a **friend**

You're never too old to learn,
but many people keep putting it off.

In college, all my
friends drank deeply at the
fountain of knowledge.
I just gargled.

Being with Mary was like being
in a telephone booth with an open
umbrella—no matter which way you
turned, you got it in the eye.

you've got a **friend**

One out of four people
in this country is mentally imbalanced.
Think of your three closest friends.
If they seem okay, then you're the one.

Gehrhart Landers

I love you no matter what you do,
but do you have to do so much of it?

Jean Illsley Clarke

I'm nuts and they all know it.
But, because we grew up together,
they understand why I turned out so
wacky. To them, I'll always be a friend
first, and a clown second. That's gold.

Denny Gimault, Comedian

you've got a **friend**

Experience is the
mistakes we like to remember.

Berta Sklansky

God has put up with a lot
from most of us.

Colette

We seldom make the
same mistake twice. Usually it's
three times or more.

Marilyn Grey

you've got a **friend**

Thanks for teaching me
right from wrong...
I especially liked
the "wrong" part.

M.D. O'Conner

My friend is someone
who helps me get in trouble.

Jimmy, age 7

Perhaps the straight and
narrow path would be wider if
more of my friends used it.

Kay Ingram

Lead me not into temptation;
I can find the way myself.

Rita Mae Brown

you've got a **friend**

I spend way too much time
searching through the Bible
for loopholes.

W.C. Fields

On the whole, human beings
want to be good, but not too good
and not quite all the time.

George Orwell

It's been my experience that folks
who have no vices have very few virtues.

Abraham Lincoln

you've got a **friend**

Life is a banquet and most
poor fools are starving to death.

Auntie Mame

I hate to eat and eat and
eat and run.

Neila Ross

I like Hostess fruit pies.
She prefers pop-up toaster tarts because
they don't require so much cooking.

Carrie Snow

you've got a **friend**

Veni, vidi, Visa.
(We came, we saw, we went shopping.)

Jan Barrett

We do not spend all our time
buying things; we spend part of it
taking them back.

Edgar Watson Howe

My friends buy just as many wigs
and makeup things as I do. They just
don't wear them all at the same time.

Dolly Parton

you've got a **friend**

The trouble with trouble is
that it always starts out like fun.

James Thurber

Opportunity knocks only once,
but temptation bangs on
the door for years.

Frank Vizzare

No one is ever old enough
to know better.

Holbrook Jackson

you've got a **friend**

My candle burns at both ends;
Where can I set it down, my friends?

The trouble with resisting temptation is
that you may not get another chance.

No, you never get any fun
out of the things you haven't done.

you've got a **friend**

Plead guilty
and often to
loving your family
and friends.

Dan Zadra

Love is nothing more than
massive liking.

Jim Cecil

The verb "to love" in Persian is
"to have a friend." "I love you" translated
literally is "I have you as a friend," and
"I don't like you" simply means
"I don't have you as a friend."

Shusha Guppy

To love anyone is nothing else
than to wish that person good.

St. Thomas Aquinas

you've got a **friend**

Loving someone allows you
to see him as God intended him.

There are many compliments
that may come to an individual in
the course of a lifetime, but there is
no higher tribute than to be loved
by those who know us best.

Insomuch as anyone
pushes you nearer to God,
he or she is your friend.

you've got a **friend**

We are taught there are seven
sacraments, but some theologians
say there should be eight.
The eighth sacrament is the
"sacrament of friendship."

Rev. Mark Connolly

In India, every time you
meet somebody, you put your hands
in front and say, "Namaste." That means,
"I honor the place in you where the
entire universe resides. I honor the
place in you where, if you are at that
place in you and I am at that place
in me, there is only one of us."

Leo Buscaglia

you've got a **friend**

We make our friends;
we make our enemies; but God
sends our next door neighbors.

G.K. Chesterton

As neighbors we began by
simply chatting over the hedge;
then one of us would squeeze
through an opening in the branches.
Eventually we'd carved out a small door
in the leaves. Rather than walking
around front to the path, one of us
would ritually crouch and crawl
through to discuss the weather
and our dreams.

Kathryn Livingston

you've got a **friend**

There's something special
about a next door neighbor—
about looking into their house at night
(not as a spy!) and seeing their
shapes moving. The presence of
my good neighbors was a comfort;
their daily comings and goings
served as a friendly counterpoint to
my own hectic schedule, and I knew
that whatever problem I might
encounter during the day
(however large or small it might be),
I could count on them for help.

Kathryn Livingston

you've got a **friend**

The scariest thing about middle
age is that we know we're going
to grow out of it.

Marcie McKinney

I'm 53 now, my little kids
are all grown up, and I am a writer.
But running has stayed the same.
Each morning, into the snows of
January, the suns of July, despite
creaking joints and bouts of menopausal
insomnia, my friends and I run together.
It's not that we love running so much.
It's that we love each other.

Cristina Hegron

you've got a **friend**

Ah, but there is no friend
like a sister.

Christina Rossetti

Dear Norma:
Am sending you twenty-five dollars.
It's going to be hard, baby—we'll probably
want money pretty bad pretty often—but
no unworthy girl ever had so many friends
as I have, and we shan't starve, because
we can borrow. I'm as crazy to see you
as if I were going to be married to you—
no one is such good pals as we are.

Edna St. Vincent Millay
inviting her sister Norma to join her in Greenwich Village

you've got a **friend**

I told you it would happen,
that our friendship was bound to end.
Although I know you care,
I cannot consider you as a friend.
Please don't try to argue,
just try to understand
that time can change people,
as the tide can change the sand.
Our friendship has been lovely,
but you see it has an end.
For now I fell in a different way,
I've fallen in love with you my friend.

Kyra, "My Friend,"
The Friendship Page

you've got a **friend**

Platonic friendship is
the interval between the
introduction and the first kiss.

Sophie Loeb

Came but for friendship
and took away love.

Thomas Moore

Funny, the biggest commitment
to friendship we can make is
sealed with just two little words:
"I do."

Steve Potter

you've got a **friend**

If I were to marry again tomorrow,
I wouldn't give up one friend. I'd take
them all with me as a sort of dowry and
tell my new husband that he was
getting a rich wife.

Merle Shain

The truth is,
friendship is every bit as sacred
and eternal as marriage.

Katherine Mansfield

you've got a **friend**

We have a great deal
more friendship than is
ever spoken. How many
persons we meet in houses,
whom yet we honor,
and who will honor us!
How many we see in the street,
or sit with in church, whom,
though silently, we warmly
rejoice to be with.
Read the language of these
wandering eye-beams.
The heart knoweth.

Ralph Waldo Emerson

you've got a **friend**

Friendship
is rhythm.
Also blues.

William "Count" Basie

Friends do not live
in harmony, merely, as some say,
but in melody.

Henry David Thoreau

True friendship is seldom serene.

Madame de Sévigné

We may not always see eye to eye,
but we can try to see heart to heart.

Sam Levenson

you've got a **friend**

Sometimes it's worse to win a fight
than to lose.

Billie Holiday

Sticks and stones may break our bones,
but words will still break our hearts.

Robert Fulghum

Misery is when your
very best friend calls you a name
she really didn't mean to call you at all.
Misery is when you call your very best
friend a name you didn't mean
to call her, either.

Langston Hughes

you've got a **friend**

Good friend, always be open
to the miracle of the second chance.

Rev. David Stier

We could be friends
Like friends are supposed to be.
You, picking up the telephone
Calling me
to come over and play,
or take a walk,
finding a place, to sit and talk
Or just goof around
Like friends do,
Me, picking up the telephone
Calling you.

Myra Cohn Livingston

you've got a **friend**

Forgiveness is the act
of admitting we are like our friends.

Christina Baldwin

I bear no grudges.
My heart is as big as the sky
and I have a mind that retains
absolutely nothing.

Bette Midler

We would like to start from scratch.
Where is scratch?

Elias Canetti

you've got a **friend**

No one can go back and make
a brand new start,
But anyone can start from here and
make a brand new end.

"Reminiscences"

The future is
sending back good wishes and
waiting with open arms.

Kobi Yamada

you've got a **friend**

People change and forget
to tell each other.

Lillian Hellman

It doesn't happen all at once.
You become. It takes a long time.

Margery Williams

The most beautiful
discovery true friends make is
that they can grow separately
without growing apart.

Elisabeth Foley

you've got a **friend**

Don't be dismayed at good-byes.
A farewell is necessary before you
can meet again. And meeting again,
after moments or lifetimes, is certain
for those who are friends.

Richard Bach

A part of you has grown in me
And so you see, it's you and me
Together forever and never apart,
Maybe in distance,
But never in heart.

Unknown

you've got a **friend**

I Feel So Miserable Without You,
It's Almost Like Having You Here

Song title by Stephen Bishop

The one good thing about
not seeing you is that I can
write you letters.

Svetlana Alliluyeva

Just put a little of
yourself in the evelope,
seal it up and send it off!

Dan Zadra

you've got a **friend**

And the song,
from beginning to end,
I found in the heart
of a friend.

Henry Wadsworth Longfellow

"We two are friends,"
tells everything.

Edward Verrall Lucas

Elizabeth Barrett Browning:
"What is the secret of your life?
Tell me, that I may make
mine beautiful, too."
Charles Kingsley: "I had a friend."

Unknown

you've got a **friend**

God evidently does not intend us
all to be rich, or powerful, or great, but
He does intend us all to be friends.

Ralph Waldo Emerson

Who, being loved, is poor?

Oscar Wilde

I awoke this morning with
devout thanksgiving for my friends,
the old and the new. I call God
"Beautiful" for these gifts.

Ralph Waldo Emerson

you've got a **friend**

I just got old
and couldn't help it.

Jean Calment, age 117

Count your nights by stars,
not shadows.
Count your days by smiles, not tears.
And on any birthday morning,
Count your age by friends,
not years.

Unknown

you've got a **friend**

They were such close friends that
even when they were two worn-out
old people, they kept on...playing
together like half-crazy puppies.

Unknown

The two old men sit in silence together,
relishing memories of the past. They are

lifelong friends and need no words to share
their thoughts. One quavers to the other,
"May you live a hundred years, and may
I live ninety-nine." The other nods his old
white head and gravely says, "Let us go
home together and drink a cup a wine."

Hsu Chi, "Old Friends"

you've got a **friend**

In our dreams
we are never eighty.
Anne Sexton

There may be snow on the roof,
but there's still a fire in the fireplace.
George Burns

We are not growing older, we are
just becoming more concentrated.
Karen Wick

you've got a **friend**

If you want
a thing done well, get a couple
of old broads to do it.

Bette Midler

Lady Astor, age 89,
planning her 90th birthday party:
"And there will be dancing!
I, for one, intend to
dance 'til dawn."

"Reminiscences"

you've got a **friend**

I'll never be a big wheel,
or a great lover, or a terrific athlete,
or a gourmet cook, or a community
leader. But one thing I can be
is a really good friend.

Dave MacNee

Dear George: Remember
no man is a failure
who has friends.
Thanks for the wings!
Love, Clarence.

Clarence, the Angel
"It's A Wonderful Life"

you've got a **friend**

Treasure each other in
the recognition that we do not know
how long we will have each other.
Joshua Liebman

I cannot forgive my
friends for dying; I do not find
these vanishing acts of theirs
at all amusing.
Logan Pearsall Smith

If you should die before me,
ask if you could bring a friend.
Stone Temple Pilots

you've got a **friend**

I shall live because there
are a few people I want
to stay with for the longest
possible time.

A.T. Salih

Someday I would like to
stand on the moon with my best friend,
look down through a quarter of a million
miles of space and say, "There certainly is
a beautiful earth out tonight."

Lt. Colonel W.H. Rankin

you've got a **friend**

I seek, dear friend, my heart's
true wish to send you, that you
may know, that far or near my
loving thoughts attend you.

"Wisdom of the Heart"

For this I bless you most.
You give much and know not
that you give at all.

Khalil Gibran

you've got a **friend**

All I want for you
is the best of everything.

Veronica Lake
Letter to a childhood friend

The good you do is not lost
though you forget it.

Jiri Masala

And could I have but one
wish this year, this only it would be:
I'd like to be the sort of friend
that you have been to me.

Edgar Guest

you've got a **friend**

When I count
my blessings,
I count you twice.

Irish proverb

Other "Gift of Inspiration" books available:

Be Happy
Remember to live, love,
laugh and learn

Be the Difference

Because of You
Celebrating the
Difference You Make

Brilliance
Uncommon voices from
uncommon women

**Commitment to
Excellence**
Celebrating the Very Best

Diversity
Celebrating the Differences

Everyone Leads
It takes each of us to make
a difference for all of us

Expect Success
Our Commitment to
Our Customer

Forever Remembered
A Gift for the Grieving Heart

I Believe in You
To your heart, your dream,
and the difference you make

Little Miracles
Cherished messages
of hope, joy, love,
kindness and courage

Never Quit
Inspiring Insights on
Courage and Commitment

Reach for the Stars
Give up the good
to go for the great

Team Works
Working Together Works

Thank You
In appreciation of you,
and all that you do

To Your Success
Thoughts to Give Wings to
Your Work and Your Dreams

Together We Can
Celebrating the power
of a team and a dream

We the People
Celebrating the
American Spirit

Welcome Home
Celebrating the Best
Place on Earth

Whatever It Takes
A Journey into the Heart
of Human Achievement

What's Next
Creating the Future Now